Dear Me

*A Letter To My
Sixteen-Year-Old Self*

EDITED BY JOSEPH GALLIANO

Dear Me

EDITED BY
JOSEPH GALLIANO

SIMON &
SCHUSTER

London · New York · Sydney · Toronto

A CBS COMPANY

First published in Great Britain in 2009 by Simon & Schuster UK Ltd,
A CBS COMPANY

1 3 5 7 9 10 8 6 4 2

Simon & Schuster UK Ltd
1st Floor
222 Gray's Inn Road
London
WC1X 8HB

www.simonandschuster.co.uk

Simon & Schuster Australia
Sydney

A CIP catalogue record for this book is available from the British Library

ISBN: 978-1-84737-766-1

Designed by Stuartpolsondesign.com
Printed and bound in Great Britain by Butler, Tanner & Dennis Ltd, Frome, Somerset

Contributors

Jake Arnott

Burt Bacharach

John Barrowman

Brenda Blethyn

Ozwald Boateng

Jeremy Bowen

Simon Callow

Alan Carr

Rosanne Cash

Julian Clary

Jackie Collins

Jenny Éclair

Tracey Emin

Hugh Fearnley-Whittingstall

Sir Ranulph Fiennes

Jane Fonda

Mark Foster

Stephen Fry

Mark Gatiss

Trisha Goddard

Julie Goodyear

Rolf Harris

Debbie Harry

Dr Christian Jessen

Little Miss Jocelyn

Sir Elton John

Peter Kay

Patsy Kensit

Lynda La Plante

Annie Lennox

Denise Lewis

Baz Luhrmann

Joanna Lumley

Lesley Manville

Hayley Mills

Alison Moyet

James Nesbitt

Paul O'Grady

Yoko Ono

Sue Perkins

Libby Purves

Anne Reid

Zandra Rhodes

Jon Ronson

Jonathan Ross

Ken Russell

Julia Sawalha

Nadia Sawalha

Nitin Sawhney

Sir Antony Sher

Liz Smith

Roberta Taylor

Emma Thompson

Adriana Trigiani

Ryan Tubridy

Archbishop Desmond Tutu

Suzanne Vega

Danny Wallace

Edmund White

Fay Weldon

Kim Wilde

Alfre Woodard

Kirsty Young

Will Young

Foreword by Sir Elton John

I was sixteen in 1963, still Reg, playing 'Roll Out The Barrel' and 'King of the Road' in the Northwood Hills Pub. But what uncharted territory lay ahead? What a journey? How could I ever have guessed how incredible it would be… and how much I could have used a kind guiding word.

When this project began and I was asked to write to that sixteen-year-old boy, it struck a real chord – what did he need to hear? What words of love could I send down to him? How much had the world changed and attitudes moved on since 1963? Reading the letters that the other contributors have written I can see that some of the same challenges faced them all. And they've all filled me with different emotions – it's really not an exaggeration to say that I was moved to laughter and to tears in turn.

Sixteen is a funny age, we are neither child nor adult: we think we know it all, but we are just kids. It is this age group in particular who have been made extremely vulnerable to HIV/AIDS. So many of them just don't know about it, and this makes them more exposed than ever, and is why the work of the Elton John AIDS Foundation is so important – in keeping the issue alive and spreading knowledge, whilst fighting the spread and mitigating the consequences of this disease, both at home and internationally. Proceeds from each copy sold of *Dear Me* is adding ammunition to our fight.

I want to thank all the contributors who have so generously given of their time in the making of this book, who have had to delve back in time and really ask themselves about their lives, their backgrounds and childhood, and who have given us some fascinating windows on their lives in a way that a simple interview never could.

A big thank-you is also due to the retailers, bookshops, supermarkets and anyone who has stocked *Dear Me*. We couldn't do this without your support.

Most of all though, a massive thanks goes to YOU who have bought the book, perhaps for yourself, your mum, dad, sister, grandmother – or even a sixteen-year-old who might like read how someone else felt at that age. There is wisdom, sadness, laughter and a warm recognition of the human condition in these pages.

I hope you enjoy these letters as much as I have.

Advice to a 16-year-old

North London
May 2009

Dear Betty

Now you are sixteen and about to leave school. You do not see any obstacles
ahead. So, hold on to your dreams because there is a long way to go.

First there is a World War that will take five years of your life. Then a
husband, who will take even more, until your children are grown up. Then
the phone call will come that will change your life.

So Dear Betty, never mind if they laugh at you – hold on to your dreams to
the very end.

Yours.
Betty Smith

THE
LETTER
CAME.

THANKS

FOR
THE
HONEY
HONEY

Liz Smith

Cornwall 2009

SUSAN.

I am calling you Susan, because I know it's my only hope of getting your attention. You hate people calling you Susan, because the name Susan conjures up a strapping, practical girl who does things like rescuing stranded Labradors from slippery escarpments in Arthur Ransome stories. Susan is not a suitable name for the pallid little Goth smoking on the school playing fields in Surrey, circa 1985.

OK. First up, and most importantly, stop worrying about wanting to kiss girls. Stop being frightened about what people may or may not think of you and just GET ON WITH KISSING THEM. If you don't, then you're going to end up being thirty-nine-years-old and feeling you haven't kissed nearly enough. Trust me, that's a terrible state of affairs.

Fact: you're never going to be a great novelist. That stuff you're writing about autumn leaves and mist rising from suburban drains - it doesn't really develop from there. Great novelists don't come from Croydon and great novelists don't have photos of themselves blind drunk and naked in nightclubs posted on the internet. If I were you, I'd stick to gurning and putting on silly outfits, which is much more your cup of tea.

Don't turn down the opportunity to wear glasses early on in your life. Firstly, they will make people think you are much cleverer than you are and secondly, they're a canny way of hiding your massive eye-bags.

Start moisturizing, particularly around the neck. It appears you HAVE inherited Granny Smith's goiter issues.

Finally, you're going to get your heart very badly broken. More than once. I'm not going to bother you with the details, there's no point. You won't listen. You'll recklessly follow your heart without a care for the dark places it might lead you towards. Good. Despite it all, good. I hope you'll always and forever bound into relationships with such hopeless idiocy and optimism.

I would say I love you. But I know you'd never believe it.

Sue xxx

PS Whatever you do, DON'T make that flippant remark to the customs official in Los Angeles in 1999. It will make you feel very differently about Marigolds.

Sue Perkins

Burt Bacharach

BURT BACHARACH

☑002

Dear   Mc—

At 16   I am so glad
I listened to my mother and kept
taking piano lessons

Burt Bacharach

www.alancarr.net

Alan Carr

Dear Me,
    You probably can't read this because you won't have your glasses on. I know you don't like wearing them but believe me - you'll grow into them.
I'll be honest with you - that isn't puppy fat!! It stays with you for the next 20 years looking a bit sorry for itself. hanging over the top of your jeans and dribbling when you giggle.
    Now I know bodyslamming your face on a caravan hook in Great Yarmouth whilst on holiday wasn't on your 'to do' list, but funnily enough the crooked, gappy, crooked, chipped toothy smile might actually be a good thing. Look!! Don't shoot the messenger - I'm trying to be positive. Anyway I've got jokes to write, presenting to do etc so will leave you to it. keep yr chin up.
    love
        Alan

    P.S. By the way, your voice doesn't break either

Mark,

I know where you are. You've run away from your father and your home. I'm writing to tell you it's all right. You'll be running (or is it searching?) for a long time. Right up front I want you to know that I know no matter what I say it won't make any difference to you. I have my own reasons for writing.

I have children now. And every day I look at them, and feel sure that they too will discover that their dad doesn't know everything; that he's fallible and one day he will, just like your father now, disappoint them.

I know it's impossible to comprehend right now, when your compass is in an angry spin, and you're running from the heroic centre of your life – the commando trainer, the fighter, the teacher, the boxer, the dancer, the funny, the leader of the Luhrmann boys… the Law. The one who, with endless ideas and enthusiasm, could do and could make anything happen.

Remember when the owner of the cinema died, and he stepped in to run the show, allowing you boys an unimaginable, all-movies pass? And how he enthused the local Rotarians to back the "crazy plan": free ballroom dancing lessons for all the children of the district. "They'll never come". But they did, in such numbers the lessons were given in shifts.

Then came the retribution to the Luhrmann boys whose father stuck his head high above the crowd, whose father had the big ideas, and whose kids "did all that stuff", the farming and the dancing, the music and photography, the boxing and the scuba diving with their crew-cuts in a world of long-haired youth. "Haven't you even heard of Slade?" Ostracised for your hair (or lack of hair), you became untouchables, weird, strange, and uncool: the Luhrmanns.

You swallowed the humiliation because that was the price of a special life, (the renaissance boys of Heron's Creek), of following your own path, and in any case you were protected by and protecting your island, the Mobil petrol station at Heron's Creek. In service to the relentless stream of travellers washed up on its shores (flotsam and jetsam of every imagining all took a stop at Len's Mobil service station) it had an overblown sense of its own magnificence: its sizzle-plate restaurant, International Snack Bar, car repairs, brother Brett's "fernery and tropical orchids", Chris's "exotic aviary" with canaries, budgerigars (and some other illegally trapped birds), and of course your own "Mark's tropical aquarium". Oh, the grandeur.

Baz Luhrmann

Then…

Your mum left. You can't really blame her: a fabulist, stranded in a town of eleven houses. Driven by that quality you and I both know only too well, that "hearing a voice whispering the answer just around each corner that you can never quite hear", but drawn forever down the yellow brick road.

Remember that terrifying day. Taking the good car, the turquoise lamp, and your baby sister. You watched your father cry, and you were frightened. An empty hollowness.

Then something incredible. A family meeting, and a plan: "we are going to tighten our belts, pull together". We were going to make it on our own. It was kind of exciting. Everything was an adventure – whether stealing gravel from the road-works or catering for the southern cross rally, or when the station was under siege from attacks of bikies, hippies, the Bee Gees, floods, fires, and hailstorms. And all the while, every second night we would wind down the two hour ribbon of highway to become ballroom dancing champions and it was here that something else happened: your father found love again.

That someone so great could change so much for a thing as stupid as a wounded heart, and the need to be loved…you will not understand that until you are older. Everything changed, because he changed. The rigid discipline and golden absolutes were no more, and the rock-solid realities turned to dust. There was a new woman, and her children. And now you're running from your father and your home. He is fallible, and you never suspected it.

Disappointed and angry, you were looking for an excuse to run to the "big smoke" – the emerald city – where they make movies and plays to the rest of the world, and life. You found your mother, then ran from the Catholic boys school (beaten because of your hair – this time too long, too curly, too Basil Brush). You ran to the streets, to the theatre, to adventure.

You will go on to make some films, meet an unusual girl, and see your father die, but not before he has laughed at the length of your hair, taken you shopping for a nose ring, explained that he has created the perfect barbeque before he tells you that he loves you. These are the things you will remember.

I am telling you this because now, at forty-six years old, I look at my own children and think of the day when they too will see their daddy has feet of clay, and go in search of their own yellow brick road. And I pray that they will one day come to understand why daddy might do what he does, even if like your own father, he does it for something as seemingly pathetic as love. I only hope they return having found themselves, before it's too late, before too much time has been wasted, to enjoy the final act when they take centre stage, our roles reversed, with them now looking out for their silly (but adorable) and adoring parents.

I have absolute confidence, my funny, sad, joyful, bright-eyed, enthusiastic, over-the-top, way-too-curly-haired (or new-wave curly-haired) sixteen-year-old-misfit-of-a-self that this won't make one jot of difference to your restless quest. As Orson Welles will intone on a vinyl record you will find at a junk shop while at drama school, "I know what it is to be young, but you don't know what it is to be old." And you'll think to yourself: "Yes I do... it's boring." But you won't know how untrue that is until you experience it for yourself.

Be safe and well,

Dear Lesley,

I'm trying very very hard here to give you the best possible advice and all I can come up with is.................

DON'T GO OUT WITH ACTORS, AND DON'T EVER EVER EVER CONSIDER MARRYING THEM, BECAUSE THEY ARE IMPOSSIBLE TO LIVE WITH AND THEY WILL TRY TO COMPROMISE YOUR LIFE, TALENT AND EVERYTHING ELSE BECAUSE THEY ARE SELF OBSESSED LOTHARIOS.

I can't think of anything else I need to warn you against dear girl, because apart from that I think you'll be just fine.

Lots of love from.

Me (you) ...... (only a little bit wiser). xx

ITV Picture Archive

Lesley Manville

Dear William,

This is you from 30 years of age! Please don't take up smoking – it is bad for your health and for your skin. Be more confident in yourself, you have more to say than you think and are wiser than you believe. Don't be afraid about who you are and what your dreams are. What you are self conscious of is not as important as you feel it is. Talk to Jeremy and confide in him, he will help you find your path. You're better looking than you think. Believe in your singing and performing, your passion for it can outweigh by miles your lack of experience. Stop playing rugby – you'll scar your knees! Follow your instincts and watch our respect.

All my love

William
x

Dear Ran

Since you're now 16, please accept this letter purely as it's meant ... friendly advice on being "an adult", the next stage up from "teenager" which begins with some folk when they're 60 and others when, like you, they're just out of short trousers and into spotty faces. (No offence but Clearasil helps hugely to avoid repelling the other sex.) I will keep my learned words of warning succinct so as not to risk boring you since you are of an age and disposition to become bored with great speed.

1. Take a bath or shower as often as possible

2. Use under-arm daily

3. Tooth-brush likewise

4. Do unto others as you would be done by

5. He who laughs last laughs longest

6. Learn the art of aggressive self-defence both physically and verbally

7. Decide what you want to be and, once you have, go for it at once and with all your might

8. Be your own man

9. Drink in moderation
    Never touch a drug
    Never smoke
    Eat only dark chocolate
    Take at least 5 fruit/veg per day

10. Accept that my advice is tedious but, once you get to 60, you'll be thankful for it.

Ran.

Sir Ranulph Fiennes

Dear Nadia,

Crikey! I'm only allowed to give you one page of advice, so I'm going to give you a funky little list of do's and don'ts, which, if you follow without question and trust everything I say, will (hopefully) result in you never needing to write a long list of advice to yourself some 29 years later! Here goes:

1) DO dump the boyfriend you're going to get in about one year's time.

2) Oh yes, and, DO dump the next couple after that. (It was a bad run of luck, take it from me.)

3) Don't be under ANY illusion that vodka is big or clever. It's just not. The only thing BIG about it, is the hangover, painfully followed by the regret!

4) Don't take up the piano – it'll end in tears for all concerned!

5) DO improve your listening skills. (People will go on and on about this, believe me!)

6) DO put money to "one side" for the taxman. He is real, he does come knocking and it's never pleasant!

7) Don't ever join a gym: it'll prove much easier to simply incinerate your cash. (This is the best financial advice you will ever get. Well, apart from number 6.)

8) DO put sun cream on your face. Just because you're "half Arabic", in no way means you won't wrinkle and sag. Believe me, if you don't use it, you will!

Nadia Sawalha

9) The grapefruit and bacon diet, the boiled egg diet, the Atkins, the cabbage soup, the kangaroo and dandelion diet and all the other half-brained diets you're going to go on, WON'T WORK and what's more, each time you fail at one, you will lose a little bit more of your soul, but regrettably nothing, absolutely nothing, from your arse!

10) The contraceptive pill WILL give you cellulite. (That's my story now, and you MUST stick to it.)

11) DO use hypnobirthing for your first labour, as childbirth hurts like f***ing hell without it. I did it with, and without. Without wasn't pretty.

12) DO say 'yes' to presenting the BBC series Perfect Partner (even though the money seems dire) or you won't end up very happily married to the rather dishy director!

13) And lastly, DO avoid trying to control people, places and things. The sooner you get this one into your thick skull, the more miraculous your life will become!

14) DO be brave, and DO accept compliments, and DO be brilliant, because in your heart you TRULY ARE.

Sent with all my love, from the older and (believe it or not) the much happier you x

P.S. In the summer of 1982 you will be on stage in very high heels at the Hampstead theatre, DO watch out for the prawn ball downstage left!

doghouse-media.co.uk

Peter Kay

Dear Peter (Age 16)

Few tips for you: Avoid stone washed denim,
Carol Farrell (as she'll break your heart...twice)
and Twin Peaks, as the ending is shit

Lots of love
Peter (Age 36)

P.S The winner of the 1992 Grand National is
'Party Politics'

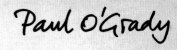

Paul O'Grady

Dear Paul,

Listen gobshite, will you give it up with the "I wish I was" malarkey, especially the one that goes how you wish you were older and shaving daily. That really pisses me off. Take it from me, wrinkles and razor-rash soon come quickly enough without you wishing your life away for them. Enjoy these worry-free, halcyon days while you can and stop fretting about the future.

Remember how that Christian Brother wrote in your school report that you were, "Born to trouble as the sparks fly upwards?" Well, he was right, so keep your wits about you when the shit starts hitting the fan, which it will, and by the bucket load.

Now, you're going to discover hair dye, so can you please think twice before going for the startling and clashing shades of red that you seem to be drawn towards. And the hair – does it have to be so bouffant? I know it's the 70s and probably very fashionable but it only makes you look like a juvenile Vera Downend from the original episodes of Crossroads.

And don't bother going to night school. 'A' level Biology is going to be of no use to you in the long run. You see, you don't become a spy for MI5, nor do you end up as a vet or a steam train driver. Sorry to disappoint you. What actually happens is this... are you ready? Look away if you don't want to know (as if!). You'll idle your time in a series of dead-end jobs until you'll find yourself one night standing in a public house dressed as an old prostitute telling filthy jokes about an imaginary sister. You'll love it though.

Oh, and speaking of scrubbers, when you finally make up your mind which bus you're going to travel on and take the route that leads you to Sadie's Bar and The Bear's Paw remember that it's not obligatory to go off with everyone who buys you half a pint of cider. Do it for nothing less than a pint, with a couple of whisky chasers if you must. Good luck,

Paul O'Grady

P.S. Don't bother investing in private pensions. They'll be worthless by the time you become an old queen.

Jackie Collins

Dear Jackie,
 At 16 you know a lot — maybe Too much !! You are a wild child ready to try anything once. But fortunatly you are street smart & wary of horny old men (30? 40?) on the make. You seem to be handling the hazards of being young in Hollywood with quite a lot of style — but you still have many things to learn. Stay away from movie stars — especially married movie stars! Stay away from drugs — not a clever scene. Do not drink Too much, avoid cigarettes & men who say "Trust me". If you can make it through your teenage years in one piece — then I feel you have a long & prestigious career ahead of you.
 Stay strong & positive & dont hurt the animals !!   XXXXs

Jackie C.

Anne Reid

Dear Anne,

You're such a _daydreamer!_
For goodness sake get a grip! Get organised!
And lose some weight, otherwise you'll always
play servants + mothers. On second thoughts
forget about acting + concentrate on singing +
the piano because that's where your heart will
always be. And spend as much time as you can
with your brothers. You'll miss them so much.
And ask Mummy + Daddy about their lives
before you came, and about your grandparents.
One day you'll long to know every detail.
And be _braver!_ You know more than you realise.
And stop thinking you're an ugly duckling.
You look _great!_ I wish I looked like you.

Love Anne. X

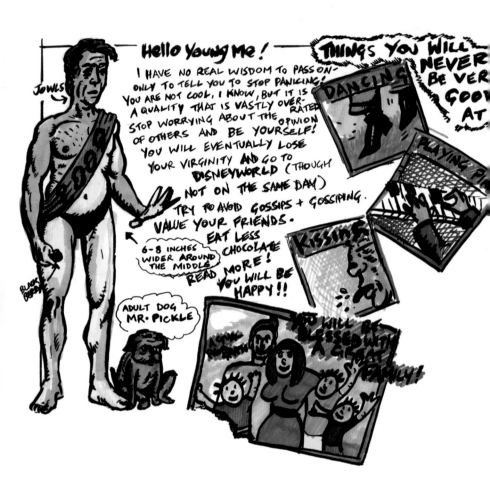

Jonathan Ross

Debbie Harry

Dear Debbie, Moon, Debeel, or Deb,

Just because you have a lot of different names, and maybe feel like there's a lot of different yous, don't be confused. Give yourself some time and all the ideas and possibilities that these names conjure up for you will become clearer to you. The pieces of the puzzle will reveal themselves and all you have to do is keep finding out what makes you feel happiest and this oftentimes will be the easiest thing for you to do. This is remarkable in itself. That the most obvious is often the best choice and can lead to something wonderful and satisfying.

In simpler words, go for it girl. 'Nothing to fear but fear itself' is such an old saying but if it helps you take a flying leap and if it's the only thing that happens, you will have the lasting, lifelong satisfaction of having made a leap. That you have the courage of your convictions and the strength within yourself to do anything, will be your core and your future can be enjoyed even when things get tough. They will get tough and they will get easy and when you look back at those times, the rough ones will often be the ones you remember best.

Dreams Do Come True. Keep dreaming,

Love, D

Alfre Woodard

Dear Bootsy
Yes, you're married hot 28 years in!

Alfre Woodard Spencer — and he is still

My darling girl, you will be considered beautiful one day. I know ha! big ass laugh. Some faces are meant for long term unfoldment and transformation. But, by then you'll have defined your beauty in ways you can't touch, your character and mainly your deeds. So, drooping physicality won't at all diminish your appeal. And relax, that whole "African" look you get

teased about, That doesn't catch The eye of guys black, brown, white or otherwise... it'll be a going currency for you one day. And by The way, you will know and befriend some Amazing Africans. And touching there, you will believe these that find favor in your face. Actually, folks will be plumping up their lips one day, like inner tubes!

Right now, know that it is ALL good. Perfection is present. You will grow into that understanding + the daily lump in throat will relax. You cannot fall off The face of The earth and you cannot fall out of

Alfre Woodard Spencer

God's love, and out of your own space. That is The only real power. So, you have absolute security right now + always. No Fear. Yes, a little rush of adrenalin, but never a need 2 fear. So, revel. Enjoy.

Be here now. Each now. And trust your instinct to 2 put you in your next proper place. Keep your heart and mind open and put yourself out in orbit... You can't imagine how glorious The sights you'll see, The hands you'll touch and The two children, beauties, who will call you Mommy with joy in Their eyes. OMG, it goes on and on and on... As does god.

your travelin' partner, self — @ 56 yrs.

Alfre

Alfre Woodard Spencer

London 20/07/09

Unfortunately, I have to break it to you that you won't ever achieve your childhood dream of becoming a pilot and you've got a few dodgy jobs ahead of you (Courier driving and filing in a council office) before you get back into swimming, but remember that in whatever you do, you should reach for the stars...you won't always reach them, but if you don't try you won't even get off the ground. Give life everything you've got! Talent alone is not enough, you will have to work hard too.

I've learnt that you get what you pay for and when you decide to get a tattoo of an English rose on your chest for the 1986 Commonwealth Games with two friends, you may want to re-think getting it done in a shop on Southend sea front! It will end up looking more like a Japanese rose and your friends' will end up with something that looks like a tomato plant and a squashed fly. This will become even more embarrassing when you start getting your chest out in public as much as I do.

You'll continue to have the odd fashion disaster (keep a special eye out for fish net tops) but for the moment you should throw away the Rupert the Bear trousers...they really don't go with deck shoes.

Continue to love Eighties music...it will come back into fashion one day.

Enjoy it, you've got some great times ahead.

Mark Foster

Alison Moyet

Dear Alla;

I'd like a friend like you. Just stop being scary they might not hit you after all. Besides, you are making people nervous and as pleased as you are with your quick tongue, you know it shames you to hurt anyone, and you do.

I like your braveness. I like how sure you are that you are meant to do something significant, regardless of not even being able to get shop work. Maybe no one has a great deal of faith in you, but everyone has their own shit going on. It's good to be self-sufficient. Stop bleating, leave well alone and know that you are a mug for wasting your education, you'd have liked an O' level. You'd have liked a comfortable relationship with punctuation.

Kim is still your best mate. She makes you happy. Mrs Paget called you a slag to your face and chucked you out for nothing. That was unreasonable. You will learn that your betters don't always have class and few have good manners. Kim's mum always liked you though, and she had her wits about her. You won't forget much. Try to.

You got money accidently, but there is still little worth buying. You got very fat a number of times and that wasn't useful always. Few people see beyond it. Beauty is king but you wont suffer age as the beautiful do. You become good-natured. You become charming. That was unexpected.

You enjoy people. Make the most of them; they thin out even as they become many.

You didn't like having a dog after all, so that was a wasted ambition.

Your beloved bike the lilac Elswick Hopper hangs in a tree in the garden, like art, the kind you said was bollocks. You'll lend it to a brother-in-law who paints it black without asking. Not best pleased. It's peeling a little now and you scratch some of the colour back when the garden is empty.

You marry and have clever children and mess up just like your parents did.

Forgive them. You will soon need forgiveness.

You will learn to read the room. You still feel everything under your skin. Nothing hurts forever. You did keep Siamese cats. I kept that promise.

Start a band. It's a lark.

You always were a lovable soul.

Alison xxxxx

Hertfordshire.

Alison x

23/6/09.

Dear Little Ant,

This is what the family call you - Little Ant - and although you don't like it, you can see their point of view : you are a tiny, dark, insignificant thing which could easily be trampled underfoot. The rest of your contemporaries, and indeed the rest of white South African males, circa 1950's and '60's, all seem to be noisy, beer-swilling, rugby-playing giants. You are quiet, shy, frightened.

You are also gay. You know you are, though it's completely secret, and you're uncomfortable with it. It makes you feel like a Martian in this macho society. Their favourite game isn't rugby actually, it's prejudice. Not just racism, which they make into the law of the land - Apartheid - but also homophobia and anti-Semitism. And you're Jewish too. When school finishes and you go into the army, compulsory at that time, you will be bullied as a "Jood", the Afrikaans word for Jew, which bears an uncomfortable similarity to the German word, and this will hurt. And then you'll wish you weren't Jewish either.

When you come to London in 1968 to study drama, you will find that another part of your identity - white South African - is hated by the entire world. You will suddenly learn about Apartheid in all its detail, everything which the Nationilist government censored back home, and you will be shocked senseless. And you will think : how could my family, who were the persecuted ones, the second-class citizens of Eastern Europe, fleeing the pogroms of the late 19th century and settling in South Africa, how could they have turned into the persecutors ?

And you will learn the answer : it might not be honourable but it's very human. If life has been hard, and now it's good, people want to enjoy it. And so they look away when atrocities happen. To do the opposite, as a small but honourable roll-call of South African Jews did (Albie Sachs, Helen Suzman, Jo Slovo, Ruth First, and others) takes a helluva lot of courage. You will feel shame that the Shers were not brave enough. You will go into yet another closet (losing your accent, telling strangers you're English), and soon you won't know where the keys are anymore

Sir Antony Sher

But then, gradually, having realised that the world is often upside down - the Old South Africa said that being gay and being Jewish were bad, while they themselves were bad beyond belief - you will start to revise your view of yourself.   You will eventually embrace being gay, and Jewish, and white South African.   You will celebrate these things, They are who you are, what you are.   In truth, you could never have been anything else.   Even though you're an actor, and pretend to be other people onstage, in real life you can only be who you are.   You will find happiness in this new state of being.   And the world will change too.   A miracle will happen in South Africa : Nelson Mandela will sweep away the old regime, without the bloodbath which everyone predicted, and bring democracy to that country.   Meanwhile Israel will create its own Apartheid, becoming ensnarled in racial prejudice and violence, and you will be appalled by all religious fundamentalism, and only call yourself a secular Jew.   Here in the U.K. a new bill will be introduced in 2005, allowing gay couples to enter into Civil Partnerships, gaining all the same rights as in a straight marriage, and you and your partner Greg Doran will be among the first to hold the ceremony.   Your party invitation will read : "After 18 years together we're legal at last!"   Legal at last.   That's quite something for someone who started life as a Martian.

And your career will turn out well too - as actor/author/artist.   In fact Little Ant will turn into Sir Antony (while friends know you as Tony).   So what I most want to say to you, my 16 year old self, is, "My boy, just hold on tight - you won't believe what lies ahead !"

With love
Tony.

Back Row: L. van Rensburg, D. Fabian, P. Riley.
Middle Row: L. Munitz, D. Irish, B. van der Merwe, A. Fagin, A. Sher.
Sitting: D. Altschuler, D. H. Gordon (Head Prefect), Mr. A. D. Dodd (Principal), M. Fletcher (Vice-Head Prefect), W. De Villiers.
PREFECTS

Archbishop Desmond Tutu

The Most Reverend Desmond M Tutu, O.M.S.G. D.D. F.K.C.
Anglican Archbishop Emeritus of Cape Town

01 August 2009

Cape Town

My dear me

Hallo, how exciting to be young. George Bernard Shaw said something like – youth is a wonderful thing - a pity it should be wasted be wasted on the young. I am not so cynical. You know, dream, be idealist, reach for stars. The sky is the limit. Your dream makes you idealistic it makes you altruistic, wanting to serve others. Enjoy it – don't be infected by the cynicism of the ancients in your midst. Your dream is realizable. You want to be doctor – then don't be daunted by the obstacles. Your parents have no money to send you to medical school, then apply for bursaries. Look for a calling that is not self serving, is intended for self aggrandizement. Remember if you have any advantages then it is to prepare you for service not privilege. God has endowed you with many gifts – develop them to the fullest and realize your potential for the sake of others. Enjoy your friends, especially your girl friends!

Hey man you have the whole of your life before you – go for it!

Much love

Your older self

Archbishop Emeritus Desmond Tutu

~r Me,
~imon and Schuster,
First Floor, 222 Gray's Inn Road,
WC1X 8HB

JOANNA LUMLEY

Dear Me,

Not long now until you leave school altogether so please try to concentrate on your work for a bit. You can't pass German 'A' level if you don't read the set books, you fool. Do one thing at a time, and do it properly. Keep up the acting but try to play women's parts now + again. Don't worry about spots: they will go. Volunteer for everything because that way lies adventure. Don't think you know everything because you've barely started. Be daring: be polite. Make your writing legible. You have 'attitude'; although this quality will be much admired in future generations it's pretty repellent so cut it out. Be kind: stop showing off. You seem to spend a lot of time laughing: that's good. You'll remember laughing like that when you're old. Do your best. Don't worry. I'll always be here. All is well; thinking of you so much, you funny young person. Keep in touch. Lots of love, xxx Me.

Joanna Lumley

Edmund White

Dear Eddie,

Almost all the things you're worried about will never happen. You think that if you don't find a lover soon no one will want you. But here I am, your older self, at age 69 embarking on a wonderful new love affair with a handsome Spaniard. You think that if you don't gain recognition as a writer (for already you want to be a writer) by the time you're 25 you'll never make it, but in fact you won't be published until you're 33 and you won't have a successful book till you're 40.

You're lucky you're a Capricorn because you'll never do anything in excess. Or rather when at age 42 you will realise you're smoking and drinking too much, you will just stop both bad habits and will never be tempted to start them again. At 16 you've already learned how to make friends and you do so almost compulsively. Only much later will you realise that friends are there to make you happy and not just for you to win over.

You'll never have any real material security and you'll always be a spendthrift, but you'll squeak by. You'll always enjoy living beyond your means in big cities—New York, Paris, Rome, San Francisco - and you'll be willing to make major sacrifices in order to live in those exciting places. Right now, at age 16, you are in the grips of a demanding sexuality, which you assume will level off over the years. I've got news for you: it won't. Fifty years from now you'll still be cruising strangers at three in the morning.

Someone once said, "First you're nervous and then you die." That, essentially, is true.

Ever yours,

Edmund.

www.edmundwhite.com

Dear Denise,

I guess you must be feeling a whole lot better after your recent performances in the heptathlon. Congratulations on finding an event that really stimulates and challenges you. I know there are some disciplines within it that you are not so good at and dislike, but I know you and one of your strengths is mental toughness so you must learn to embrace the things you don't like, this will give you an advantage going forward and turn your biggest weakness in to your greatest strength.

Your aim right now should not be trying to be the best Junior athlete it should be to learn your trade and not worry about everyone else. Remember why you wanted to do this in the first place it was never about anyone else. How far can you push yourself? If you hold on to this thought throughout your career I am certain you will unlock the potential that you don't realize you have yet.

I know you and your mom have not been getting on very well recently but don't take that it heart. She only wants the best for you and she can't see your destiny nor can she see that her determination and courage are within you. One day she will be bursting with pride and the whole world will see it.

I hope this letter gives you the peace of mind that you have been looking for knowing that I believe in you. So enjoy your life and be true to yourself always.

Love.

Denise
x x

Danny Wallace

Dear Daniel

Hello there! It's me! You! Us!

I am writing to you from the future. It is great here. My robot butler says hello, and once I've landed this jetpack on my iHome I'll say hello back.

I am 32 now, which is twice your age. This means I have twice your experience! Twice your knowledge! I've kissed twice as many girls! (2!!!)

Sadly, I am also twice your size.

But on the subject of girls, I am writing to warn you. You know that girl you kissed recently near the leisure centre in town? Your first? In a few months' time, it will become apparent that she plays for her own team. Do not panic. Despite what Alec and Chris will tell you, you did *not* do this.

16
+16
____
32
✓

Anyway, after you turn that girl into a lesbian (sorry), you will encounter what you will come to know as an extended dry patch. Again, do not panic. After that, you will be fighting them off. (This may be a lie).

One thing: can I suggest you start learning the guitar now, as that will make us seem a lot cooler at university, when we end up sharing a flat with some musicians, and all we can really do to join in of an evening is bang a toaster with a spoon. This will do your extended dry patch absolutely no good whatsoever. But don't just learn the stuff you're into now. No one's going to be interested in acoustic versions of Proclaimers tracks, or Dancin' On The Ceiling. You're going to have to start pretending you're interested in Jeff Buckley, and Bob Dylan.

Google them.

Oh hang on, you can't.

Actually, buy shares in Google. That should sort just about everything out.

Yours,

You.

. VITAL! MAKE SURE YOU STAY IN ON THE NIGHT OF THE 16/6/03

THIS IS NOT TECHNICALLY MUSIC

Dear Me,

Look at you-so confident-so insecure-so cocky-so very shy.

Think you know it all- you know bugger all. You'd no idea for instance that you'd be pregnant at 17yrs old-just one year after this photo was taken. How stupid was that. Your first real boyfriend, quite a few years older than you and you still a virgin. What a bloody shock that was, wasn't it lady. Straight into a red hot bath and a bottle of gin to drink- scalded and lots of retching but still pregnant.

Oh the shame-the embarrassment it brought on the family- the anger and the disgust, not so cocky now-are you.

After the shotgun wedding -You wore blue-as a mark of shame-no white for you- that was only for virgins then.

He buggered off to Australia and left you holding the baby-poor cow. Couldn't blame him really- he wanted to make a fresh start- a new life for himself. He said "look after yourself" "Tara" and you never heard from him ever again.

But that's one of the things that made you stand up and be counted and with a resolve of steel-WORK-WORK-WORK for a better future for your son and you and your Mam & Dad.

And when you and your son stood in Buckingham Palace and you received an MBE for services to Television & Drama in 1996 it felt like a dream- didn't it ? But it wasn't- it was true.

Yes, at times, it's been a Bumpy Ride and Yes- you've had to keep your seat belt fastened.

You've led a leopard skin life and it never seems to go out of fashion. It just goes round and round in circles. But it goes so quickly. Time really does fly- it's not to be wasted.

Thank God for that wonderful sense of humour that was a gift from birth- it's stood you in good stead and kept your feet firmly on the ground. You've never forgotten your roots, in fact you still live in the same Lancashire Cotton Town where you were born.

Look at you-so confident – so insecure – so cocky – so very shy.

Leopards never change their spots.

Love-Just Julie xxx

Julie Goodyear

JOHNBARROWMAN

johnbarrowman.com

Sent from my car driving to Cardiff after concert at London's Royal Albert Hall on June 1st, 2009.

John, please turn off 'Dynasty' and read this.

1. I'm starting with this one because it will disappoint you. There are no flying cars in the future. No hovercrafts zipping up walls, no supersonic vehicles shooting out of garages at rocket speeds. Not happening. You, though, have kept up your passion for cars of all shapes and sizes and in the future you own some really cool ones.

2. Dream big, work hard, and floss everyday. Trust me. All three will pay off.

3. Continue to surround yourself with people who nurture your talents. Drop the ones who don't have passion or dreams.

4. Finally, and keep this one to yourself. Remember the story you read in the *Chicago Tribune* about the two guys who invented an amazing piece of technology in their garages in California a few years ago? Despite their company's fruity name, insist that dad buy all the stock he can afford.

John Barrowman

LETTER TO 16-YEAR-OLD SELF – JENNY ÉCLAIR

Oh just go for it, nothing I would say would make any difference. You wouldn't listen, or you'd pretend to but you'd be thinking about getting off with someone – or whether that new perm is a disaster (it is, but it will look ok when it's 'dropped' a bit)

OK, for starters, it might be a good idea if you started actually trying to learn something at school. You're going to have one big fat chip on your shoulder about your rubbish education in the future. Secretly of course, I'm on your side, those teachers are crap and you're not as thick as some people think.

Stop sun-bathing, it won't work, fake tan is going to get better, just be patient and stop eating seconds, you'll only get really fat and then waste a few years being anorexic - which I promise you will be v.v.v. dull. Be nicer to your grandparents, they won't live forever, they have stories to tell. Take better care of your Nanna's diary, you will be gutted when you lose it. In fact you could do with being a bit kinder to your entire family, give them all a break now and again, weirdly you will end up living round the corner from your sister - ha, who'd have thought? And your brother won't be a nuisance forever. As for your parents, God, you are lucky.

Take more photos, one day you will want to be reminded of how young you were.

Don't just sleep with boys because you can't be bothered to say 'No'.

One day you will shock yourself, you will be more fortunate than you deserve to be, the risks you will take make me feel sick when I remember them - I can't believe you will get away with as much as you do! There are some dreary times ahead, some horrible bed-sits and terrible mistakes, you're going to have to work your arse off but there are some fantastic surprises and yes the three things you really want you will get.

Phew.

Julian Clary

Camden, London, July 2009

Dear Julian,

At the moment you are a willowy virgin who has never had an alcoholic drink and wears Marks and Spencer's slacks and sensible shoes. You think you'd like to be a vet. All this will change.

It's hard to swallow, but in a few years time you will swan around in black rubber consuming men like After Eight Mints. You will earn a living making jokes about gay sex in all its glorious variations. Some people will like you but the Daily Mail will not.

You have a tendency to worry and will spend several uncomfortable years plagued by panic attacks. But rest assured that the Universe will always protect you.

Your partner Christopher and your dear friend Stephen will be taken from you by AIDS, but you will never stop thinking of them and you will always love them.

Whenever you are miserable go out and find a homeless puppy. Love will come and find you again when you are ready.

You are set to have a happy and unusual life. Comedy, television shows, book writing – all this excitement awaits you. Although you can't dance you will become a ballroom dancer and although you can't sing you will star in a West End Musical. Don't try and figure this out, just go with the flow.

Peace and salutations,

x

Me x

P.S. If anyone offers you Crystal Meth at a party make your excuses and leave.

julianclary.co.uk

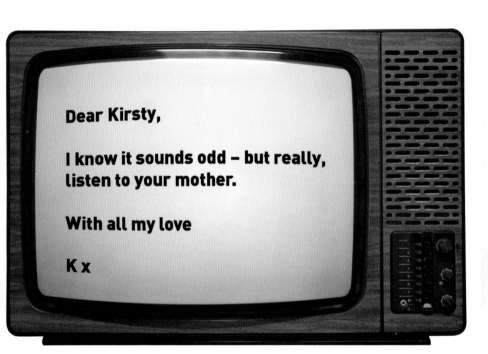

Dear Kirsty,

I know it sounds odd – but really, listen to your mother.

With all my love

K x

Kirsty Young

National Theatre

1st.

Brenda Blethyn

the Royal Harbour Hotel
Nelson Crescent
Ramsgate
Kent CT11 9JF
United Kingdom

Email: info@royalharbourhotel.co.uk
Web: www.royalharbourhotel.co.uk

25 July 2009

Dear Brenda,

So you don't have a proper pair of shoes and your clothes aren't very fashionable, but believe me, things will get a whole lot better. And there's nothing wrong with being shy even though you do your best to cover for it. Your grades at college weren't very good in the first year were they? but that's only because you are worrying about mum and dad. I know they're much older than your friends' parents and seem to be arguing a lot lately, all parents do, but I'll bet not everyone's parents laugh as much together as yours do. So please stop being so morbid because they're going to be around for a long time yet.

Would you believe me if I said your life was going to take a different course altogether from the one you a currently planning, (although the shorthand and typing will come in very handy whatever you do – my hands are whizzing across the keyboard now – especially if you ever come to write a book!) It's not such a far-fetched idea.

Listen Brenda, don't try so hard to be liked. The sooner you learn that some people won't like you, the better. And remember that your opinion is just as valuable as anybody's. Don't be embarrassed if you get things wrong. Everybody gets things wrong. Dad was right when he said there's nothing wrong with failure, only with not trying.

Oh dearest Brenda, I know you will never ask for the moon and stars, and you are blessed for it. You will work hard in life but I promise you that if you stand on tippy-toes you will reach whatever you crave. Put the chocolate on the top shelf.

And finally, eschew pretension. If you want any more advice little Bren, you can contact me via my agent Sally Long-Innes at Independent Talent, London.

Keep smiling,

With affection
Brenda Blethyn

Dear Jake,

I'm writing to you from the future to let you know that though you are going through a hard time at the moment, things will get better. I know you feel a failure: dropping out of school, not knowing what to do with yourself, dazed and confused by all your emotions and desires. But I want you to know that what other people see as your mistakes in life will all contribute to your success. Everything seems to be going wrong at the moment but you will get what you want. There will be highs and lows ahead but you will become the person that you always wanted to be. I won't spoil any surprises because I know you've never wanted to know exactly what's going to happen. You always were, and continue to be, unpredictable.

Just remember: being queer is a blessing not a curse. Loving your own sex as well as the opposite isn't a perversion, it's a generosity of spirit. I know you're scared of not being normal but don't be. You're extraordinary, that's all, fabulous even. And you're not alone. Don't worry, you'll find plenty of people like you out there in the world. You might not feel so happy inside right now but don't be so hard on yourself. I'd like to say thanks for being who you are at your age. All the trouble you're going through means that I can be who I am now. Just trust your instincts and follow your nature, wherever it leads. And I'll try to stay true to all your hopes and dreams.

Much love,

Jake x

Susi Arnott

Jake Arnott

Dearest absurd child,

I hope you are well. I know you are not.

As it happens you wrote in 1973 a letter to your future self and it is high time that your future self had the decency to write back. You declared in that letter (reproduced in your 1997 autobiography Moab Is My Washpot) that "everything I feel now as an adolescent is true". You went on to affirm that if ever you dared in later life to repudiate, deny or mock your 16-year-old self it would be a lie, a traducing, treasonable lie, a crime against adolescence. "This is who I am," you wrote. "Each day that passes I grow away from my true self. Every inch I take towards adulthood is a betrayal." Oh, lord love you, Stephen. How I admire your arrogance and rage and misery. How pure and righteous and right they are and how passionately storm-drenched was your adolescence. How filled with true feeling, fury, despair, joy, anxiety, shame, pride and above all, supremely above all, how overpowered it was by Love. My eyes fill with tears just to think of you. Of me. Tears splash onto my keyboard now. I am perhaps happier now than I have ever been and yet I cannot but recognise that I would trade all that I am to be you, the eternally unhappy, nervous, wild, wondering and despairing 16-year-old Stephen, angry, angst-ridden and awkward but alive. Because you know how to feel and knowing how to feel is more important than how you feel. Deadness of soul is the only unpardonable crime and if there is one thing happiness can do, it is mask deadness of soul.

I finally know now, as I easily knew then, that the most important thing is love. It doesn't matter in the slightest whether that love is for someone of your own sex or not. Gay issues are important and I shall come to them in a moment, but they shrivel like a salted snail when compared to the towering question of love. (By the way, Stephen, I believe the Bay City Rollers have recently been claiming, "If the question is love, the answer is 'yes'". They are quite wrong. If the question is love, the answer is "I wish I fucking knew" – as one of their number will discover to his cost all too soon.) Gay people sometimes believe (to this very day, would you credit it, young Stephen?) that the preponderance of obstacles and terrors they encounter in their lives and relationships are intimately connected with the fact of their being gay: as it happens at least 90% of their problems are to do with Love and Love Alone: the lack of it, the denial of it, the inequality of it, the missed reciprocity in it, the horrors and heartaches of it. Love cold, love hot, love fresh, love stale, love scorned, love missed, love denied, love betrayed…

the Great Joke of sexuality is that these problems bedevil straight people just as much as gay. The 10% of extra suffering and complexity that uniquely confronts the gay is certainly not incidental or trifling, but it must be understood that Love Comes First. This is tough for straight people to work out.

(By the way, when I say gay, I mean queer, homosexual, poof, fairy, faggot, flake, noun and adjective – although I maintain gay is actually, like me and you and everyone, a verb. Well, we can argue that another day, the point is that Gay is the Word and it is Ours. And when I say gay [triple relative clause coming], I actually mean LGBT, which I shan't bother to explain to you but you should know is an unwieldy block of letters which in its clumsy, endearing and admirably bien pensant way embraces all those with different sexual impulses who can be, for the sake of convenience, fellowship, respect and love, counted as one proud and happy band of brothers and sisters [and much in between, but again I don't want to bamboozle you at this stage]. So take the word "gay" from hereon in to mean the wild, huddled masses yearning to be free who cluster under a notional Statue of Gay Liberty.)

Yes, to return to my thread, yes. Straight people have it so tough. They are encouraged by culture and society to believe that their sexual impulses are the norm and therefore when their affairs of the heart and loins go wrong (as they certainly will), when they are inevitably flummoxed, distraught and defeated by love, they are forced to believe that it must be their fault. We gays at least have the advantage of being brought up to expect the world of love to be imponderably and unmanageably difficult for we are perverted freaks and sick aberrations of nature, but they – poor normal lambs – naturally find it harder to understand why, in Lysander's words, "the course of true love never did run smooth."

Gay life has the straightforward advantage of each partner being the same species of the other. Sexual availability, so long an impossible dream in your age, becomes the norm in the late 70s and early 80s, only to be shattered by a new Disease whose horrors you cannot even imagine.

You would little believe that I can say to you now across the gap of 35 years that we are the blessed ones. The people of Britain are happy (or not) because of Tolpuddle Martyrs, Chartists, Infantry Regiments any number of ancestors who made the world more comfortable for them. And we, gay people, are happy now (or not) in large part thanks to Stonewall rioters, Harvey Milk, Dennis Lemon, Gay News, Ian McKellen, Edwina Currie (true) et al and the battered bodies of bullied, beaten and abused gay men and women who stood up to be counted and refused to apologise for the way they were.

It has given us something we never thought to have: Pride. For a thousand years Shame was our lot and now, turning on a sixpence, we have arrived at Pride – without even it seems an intervening period of well-it's-okay-I-suppose-wouldn't-have-chosen-it-but-there-you-go. Who'd a thought it?

I now what you are doing now, young Stephen. It's February 1973. You are in the library, cross-referencing bibliographies so that you can find more and more examples of queer people in history, art and literature against whom you can hope to validate yourself. Leonardo, Tchaikovsky, Wilde, Barons Corvo and von Gloden, Robin Maugham, T. C. Worsely, "An Englishman", Jean Genet, Cavafy, Montherland, Roger Peyrefitte, Mary Renault, Michael Campbell, Michael Davies, Angus Stewart, Gore Vidal, John Rechy, William Burroughs. And so many great spirits really do confirm that hope! It emboldens you to know that such a number of brilliant (if often doomed) souls shared the same impulse and desires as you. I know the index-card waltz of (auto)biographies, poems and novels you are dancing: those same names are still so close to the surface of my mind nearly four decades later. Novels, poetry and the worlds of art and ideas are opening up in front of you almost incidentally. You spend all your time in the library yearning to be told that you are not alone and an unlooked for side-effect of this just happens to be a real education achieved in a private school designed for philistine bumpkins. Being born queer has given you, by mistake, a fantastic advantage over the rugger playing ordinaries who surround you. But those rugger playing ordinaries have souls too. And you should know that. I know you cannot believe it now. They seem so secure, so assured, so blessedly normal. They gave Cuthbert Worsley the Kipling-derived title of his overwhelmingly important (to you) autobiography The Flannelled Fool "these are the men that have lost their soul/The flannelled fool at the wicket/And the muddied oaf at the goal". You look down at the fools almost as much as you fear them. The ordinary people, the ones whose path through life is guaranteed. They won't have to spend their days in public libraries, public lavatories and public courts ashamed, spurned and reviled. All queer people have are small wood portioned space: library shelves, lavatory stalls, video booths and the Dock. There is no internet. No Gay News. No Gay Chatlines. No Men Seeking Men Personals. No Out and Proud Celebs. Just a world of shame and secrecy.

Somehow, as you age, a miracle will be wrought. You will begin by descending deeper into the depths: expulsion, crime and prison – nothing really to do with being gay, but everything to do with love and your inability to cope with it. Yet you will, as the Regency rakes used to say, "make a recover" and find yourself up at university where it will be astonishingly easy to be open about your sexuality. No great trick, for the university is Cambridge, long a hotbed of righteous tolerance, spiritual heavy petting and homo hysteria. You will emerge from Cambridge and enter a world where being 'out' is no big deal, although a puzzlingly small number of your coevals will find it as easy as you to emerge from the shadows. Never overlook how wonderful your parents are. Before you damn anyone for failing to come out, look to their parents. The answer almost always lies there. Oh how lucky in that department, as in so many, you are, young Stephen.

But don't kid yourself. For millions of teenagers around Britain and everywhere else it is still 1973 and time will go backwards as each decade passes until we arrive at now, where for many it is now 1573. Taunts, beatings and punishment await gay people the world over in playgrounds and execution grounds (the distance between which is measured by nothing more than political constitutions and human will). Yes, you will grow to be a very, very, very, very lucky man who is able to express his nature out loud without fear of hatred or reprisal from any except the most deluded, demented and sad. But that is a small battle won. A whole theatre of war remains. This theatre of war is bigger than the simple issue of being gay, just as the question of love swamps the question of mere sexuality. For alongside sexual politics the entire achievement of the enlightenment (which led inter alia to gay liberation) is under threat like never before. The cruel, hypocritical and loveless hand of religion and absolutism has fallen on the world once more. And this time the moral majority (which is neither) has cantingly pirated the fruits of an empirical science it professes to despise and is using the technological power unloosed by that very science to denigrate, anathematise and outlaw the dearly, painfully won freedoms of us, the other, the strange, the outside.

So my message from the future is twofold. Fear not, young Stephen, your life will unfold in richer, more accepted and happier ways that you ever dared hope. But be wary, for the most basic tenets of rationalism, openness and freedom that nourish you now and seem so unassailable are about to be harried and besieged by malevolent, mad and medieval, minds. You poor dear, dear thing. Look at you weltering in your misery. The extraordinary truth is that you want to stay there. Unlike so many of the young, you do not yearn for adulthood, pubs and car keys. You want to stay where you are, in the Republic of Pubescence, where feeling has primacy and pain is beautiful. And you know what...?

I think you are right.

All my love

Stephen

xxx

Stephen+35

Patsy Kensit

16th July 2009
Highgate
London

Dear 16 year old Patsy,

You adore music more than anything in the world, you have
a great passion for rock and roll ..... but that doesn't mean
you have to marry the lead singer of every band you ever
had a poster of, on your bedroom wall.

love
your older you!
Patsy x.

Rosanne Cash

New York City, June 2009

Dear Rosanne,

You deserve a lot better than the guy you are going to meet next year. When you do meet him, just let him pass, like he was a ghost. Don't even open the door. Don't even start the conversation. He's angry and ignorant (the worst possible combination of character defects) and if you take up with him, it will take you a long time to get back to your real self. You are not one to take advice, but trust me on this. You need to slam the door on anyone who doesn't respect you and this is the moment to do it for the first time.

Now that I've alarmed you with a warning, I want you to know that you will get to do most of the things you want in your life, and some you haven't even considered. (Forget about dancing and medicine. You're not cut out for either, and you'll find that although you have a lot of options, you don't have all options. You'll have to pare your dreams down to what you're actually suited for. You can always go to the ballet and read medical mysteries.) You will travel, and fall in love, and have children, and do the two things you want most in the world: write and make music. You'll get over your stage fright and your writer's insecurity and both writing and performing will be fulfilling and exciting beyond what you can now imagine. I would practice the piano more, if I were you. (Which I am). It's going to come in handy later on. And you're not going to pick up the guitar for another two years—what are you waiting for? An engraved invitation?

Don't ever chew gum again after this moment. It's unseemly.
Ask your parents for advice once in awhile. Really. They are not that old.
Sports are great for reducing stress, but wandering the beach in a bikini for an entire day is overrated.
Try to remember that overwhelming feelings are the raw material of great art. But you still have to keep your side of the street clean in love and marriage.
Don't blame anyone for anything, ever. It's also unseemly.

Everything is not going to be good, but everything will be perfect.
The best is coming up.

Love,
Your Middle Aged Self (who has a tremendous amount of affection for you, and covets the elasticity of your skin)

[signature]

p.s. Those polka-dotted bellbottoms will come back in style. Will you please save them for me?

Greenwich Village, NYC 2009-07-29

Dear Adri,

There is no such thing as waterproof mascara.
Acne at 16 means no wrinkles at 40.
One good man is enough.
The stars over the Isle of Capri glitter the most.
The root of your front tooth will eventually die.
New York City is even better than you dreamed it would be.
Do not pray to be pretty, be grateful you're funny.
The beds really are better at the Four Seasons.
Baton twirling is not a skill you need later in life.
Never pluck your eyebrows.
The moon over Big Stone Gap, Virginia, is the most beautiful
Read Jackie Collins before you go to Hollywood.
16 is the new... toddler.
You will miss your grandmothers more than you dreaded
losing them.
Get the epidural.
Listen to Emma Thompson about dieting.

Love, love and more love,
    xoxo
    Adriana

Adriana Trigiani

Dear Kim

I write this letter at the age of 48. I know that sounds ancient to you, but I still wear tight(ish) black jeans and leather jackets!

Although I would love to tell you some wonderful details about your life to come, I won't; suffice to say that all your dreams will come true, although not all in exactly the way you imagine and not necessarily when you want them to either.

Trust in the people and things you love for they will be a constant in your life. Don't be surprised, however, if the people and things you love sometimes hurt you – all the best things in life hurt a little bit from time to time.

Never be afraid to jump in at the deep end – you will always keep your head above water, even when you think you've forgotten how to swim.

Always counter jealousy and anger with love and compassion. This is a hard lesson to learn and over the years to come you will both succeed and fail in equal measure.

Trust your intuition, it will never let you down, and treat success and failure as the imposters they both are.

Have fun, laugh a lot and don't worry so, my complicated girl.

Love Kim

Kim Wilde

p.s Verbena bonariensis

www.kimwilde.com

Kim Wilde

* Former.

To embarrassing
to confess, even now!

Dear 16-year-old Jon, Ronson

There's no point in pussyfooting around the
subject: you are having a really crap time
somehow, it has all fallen apart. ~~scribbles~~ ~~scribbles~~
~~scribbles scribbles scribbles scribbles scribbles~~
~~scribbles~~ * your friends have just
thrown you in the lake. The other day
you saw your best friend in a cafe, with
the girl you're besotted with, and so you went
in to say hello, and you saw their reflection
in the mirror. It said, "OH GOD! Him!"

Jon Ronson

You are persistantly bullied. You had a party when your Parents were away and gatecrashers smashed up the house. Someone asked you what it was like to be you and you said: "It's fine. I've built a thick wall around myself and I'm deep inside it."

You probably think all this has no Point. But let me tell you, it DOES. It has a ~~point~~ Point. Somehow, within all of This, within your isolation, something ~~something~~ is happening to you. You are becoming a WRITER. Maybe you need this pain to be able to see the world clearly — in all it's absurdities — from the outside. You're becoming a funny writer, and in 2 years you'll leave CARDIFF and the rest of your life will be amazing.

P.S. IN THE PHOTO YOU ARE THIS. BUT YOU ARE TOYO-ING

Love JON xxx

March 8th 2009.

Atlanta.

Dear Reg, you are a very young 16. You know nothing about sex — you don't even know what a queer is. Trust me when I tell you — you are 'queer', you are a gay boy. I made the mistake of not having ~~sex~~ until I was 23! I loved being with another man and felt relieved that I finally knew who I was. I made the mistake ~~because~~ of falling in love too ~~soon~~ because I was naive and romantic. My advice to you is never to close love — it will find you when you least expect it. Have Fun, have lots of safe sex and enjoy your ~~sexuality~~. Be proud of who you are and, as you get older and wiser ~~fight~~ for gay rights — I'm 46 years OLDER than you are, and we have a long way to go. In certain countries we are still not treated as equals, especially by the so-called 'Christian' Church. I made a lot of mistakes. Stay away from drugs ~~they~~ they're a waste of time. Stand up for every human being's rights. Be loving, kind and strong. Set an example. You're going to have a hell of a life!! Love you Elton x
PS. CHANGE YOUR NAME

Sir Elton John

Menorca 2009

HELLO ROB

Dear Rob,

I've started this letter so many times. It's far more difficult than I imagined. Through the myopic fog of history, and believe me that's no joke if you could see me struggling with numerous pairs of specs these days, I can just about focus on you.

Sixteen-year-old Rob, striding down the Waterloo Road, eight o'clock in the morning and munching on a bar of fruit and nut chocolate for breakfast. Eager to start another day as the office junior and play with the switchboard. Trying your best to sound un-cockney and a bit more lady-like as you answer each call with: "Good morning, Bradley Pulverizer... how may I help you?"

I've used a couple of those memories in a book. How about that then? Don't worry, the geography and names were changed, your big feet and flat chest never mentioned.

This letter is supposed to be about advice but frankly, I'm a bit reluctant. Our opinionated clan, relentlessly fired out their judgements and I don't reckon it's healthy to absorb much more. You cogitating on their every word will not promise the recipe for a wonderful, exciting life.

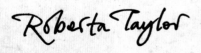
Roberta Taylor

Think about it, Rob. Between the lot of them, they managed to break almost every one of the so called "Ten Commandments", let alone a thousand others they managed to chase into the tablets. And we're not talking religion here.

"It's the principle of the thing", they holler.

Well, principles, morality, should be owned by the individual. It's not some tribal inheritance. Listen, then filter. Work it out for yourself. I know they want to protect you from their own fuck-ups but the times they are a-changing, m'dear. And not before time.

That handsome young man you are working with at the moment DOES fancy you, you know. Black glossy important hair, violet eyes, exotically American. But he has everything against him, as far as Mum is concerned. And no, you can't go out on a date with him.

If he's so good looking, with time and money to spend a year off poodling around Europe, visiting all his father's companies and heir to the Bradley Pulverizer throne, why should he be interested in you? That's what she wants you to ponder on. Rich, gorgeous and, to put the tin hat on it, American. Americans, with their easy going chat-up lines. She tells you about the war, and how many bastard babies were left behind when the Yanks toddled off back home. Why would he be interested in you?

Maybe he was lonely? Maybe because you were the nearest in age that he knew in London?

I can see you looking out of your bedroom window, trying to imagine how much bigger, quieter or louder, his life might be in comparison to yours. Too late now, and couldn't matter less.

Funny isn't it, how any local boy would be given the once over but this one would never get the invite. I can tell you now, it was because Mum was too defensive about her own life and surroundings, about her intellect or lack of it. Scared of losing you to some alien trespasser, that this new world of yours would turn your head and diminish you.

She was frightened of sex, money and thievery. That somehow, each had to be involved with the other. Marrying for money was a whore's game, sex for sex's sake was even more depressing, resulting in both cases, as some theft of the soul. It's going to take you a few years to get over those ideas, but you will eventually.

I have to tell you, everything Mum said and did, was out of a great passion for you and your hopeful future; that your life must be better and not a carbon copy of her own. But unwittingly, she crowned you with a shame that was not yours to bear.

Right at the beginning of this letter, I mentioned I was a bit reluctant about advice-giving, but I'm coming around to it, the closer I see you.

That old chestnut, "boys are only after one thing, if they can get there", is a kind of truth, but the squashy bits of life can be hotter and funnier than you can fathom at the moment. So enjoy the wolf-whistles... they stopped for me quite some time ago... enjoy the under-the-jumper groping. I recommend no more than five minutes for the groping, then hop it. On a bus, if you can.

By the way, within the next eighteen months you won't be virgo intacta anymore. Just thought I'd mention it. The gift from that particular fumble has now made you/me, a grandmother.

To be fair, maybe the teenage sex muddles, "Do I look tarty? Do I look easy?", would have happened anyway. With or without the family legacy.

But some things, I am very grateful for. What started out as a mistrust of everything and everyone, developed into a pretty fine shit detector.

1. Not passing any exams doesn't prevent you from being informed, or smart.
2. "Romance" is a prissy excuse for ardour and real love.
3. Big feet can be quite an advantage sometimes. You won't get blown over in a strong wind.
4. Frocks hang better on a flat chest.

Of course, I could be wrong so don't hang on to my every word.

Hugs and a far-away wave

Rob x

P.S. 5. Especially, to have the one thing denied most women of the previous generation... good mates and loyalty.

Trisha Goddard

Dear Trisha,

The most important thing you can do is to trust your intuition. People will used veiled put-downs like 'You've got a good imagination', or insist 'you've got things wrong. You haven't. It's just that your emotional honesty scares them.

Don't worry about not fitting in. It means you'll never be a sheep. Not belonging will give you the freedom to follow your dreams instead of the crowd. Never be afraid to be the first to achieve something — someone has to be.

One day there'll be a black President. So believe me, Nichelle Nichols playing Lt. Uhura on 'Star Trek' is just the beginning!

Continue to live life to the full and remember shit happens — it's how you handle it and what you learn from it that matters.

One day you'll meet someone who loves & accepts you purely for who you are — not for what you do. Keep trying to win praise from your dad, because although you'll never ever get it, you'll become wealthy and successful as a result. After all, lots of poo sure helps the roses grow!

Lastly — two VERY important things. You're not mad. He's not your father. Have courage and confront your mother before she gets trapped in the lies forever.

And you know that signature you've been practising in your schoolbooks since you were twelve? It'll never change!

Love

trishatv.com

Simon Callow

Dear Simon

Thank you for your last letter. I see that things
are pretty hellish for you although, thank God,
you seem to be able to laugh about it. I'm not
entirely surprised that the Sex Thing, as you call
it, looms so large, though from this perspective
it looks as if it's part of a larger question: where
will you find like-minded people? Relax: you
will. Friendship will be the core of your life. As
for the Sex Thing, I see that the problem is not just
whether you'll ever met another gay man (gay:
that's our word for homosexual, faggot, poove, pervert,
all of which words will have withered away by the
time you're a grown man) but that even if you
do, he'd run a mile from you.

You need to bear two things in mind: first, that
though (for all the reasons you mentioned) you find yourself deeply unattractive, you are, in fact, quite well
put together, and, given a little intelligent work on
yourself, you could be positively sexy. I know you
loathe sport for all the right reasons, but I wish you
could find one you liked: the interchange with other
human beings on a physical level, the sheer pleasure
of romping around as a young human animal —

– these things put you in life. Which is where you need to be. Out of your head, and in your life.

Second, you must grasp the fact that in matters of sexual desire, it is opposites that attract. You think that tall, slim, beautiful people only want to have affairs with tall, slim, beautiful people. Narcissists are, of course, everywhere among us, but more often than not – as the divine Socrates whom you have just so joyfully discovered avers – people are looking for lovers who will complete them, not duplicate them. – As for your family, who (quite understandably) drive you mad, try to forgive them. It's not easy being them. Remember what Oscar Wilde said: it is the duty of the young to set a good example to their elders.

The most important thing of all is not to live in fear. Follow your impulses. You will only ever regret the things you didn't do, never the things you did. Know that the human mechanism, of which you are a healthy example, is essentially self-regulating: you will know when you are doing something to excess. And then you will stop. You want to live, after all.

You may not feel it now, but you are, and you always have been, loved. The loving was sometimes misguided and misplaced and confused and confusing, but it was love: and this means that you will be able to love others. And in the end, that will be what your life will be about. And insofar as it is ~~that~~ about that, you will have succeeded.

Write soon: much love Simon

Zandra Rhodes

Dear Younger Self,
    What words of wisdom can
I give you?
    Most important enjoy
your work at school.
Don't grow up too fast!
Learn, learn, learn!
There is so little time later.
    I can't remember being
16!*! Only when I look
at the photos am I reminded.
The pictures look idyllic
but I know I felt insecure with
an inferiority complex and I was
sensitive.
    Always put your work, learning
and homework first before
everything. Remember you are
building your life.
    Take no notice of what others
say because you are working...
, tables turn later in life!*!
Good, Better, Best never let it rest
till your good is better & your better Best!

To a 16-Year-Old Ken Russell
from an 82-year-old Ken Russell

Dear Brush,

The Repeal of the Corn Laws is not going to be that essential for you to remember, so relax if you can.

And there aren't any people on the underside of the puddle, so you can stop looking. Your intuition is right, though – this world is not what it seems.

Just about all of it is upside down and inside out. It's the grandest illusion you ever saw – much of it designed to trick you into thinking you're only making one mistake after another. Or that love and truth aren't the main things. Don't fall for the distortions in the fun house mirrors – you'll know the real thing when you see it. The streak of a star across the night sky, the vibration of the train roaring through St Denys' station – your job is to hold onto a vision for which there are no words.

When the kids make fun of you or your accent, know it's not that important. You'll be good at some games, and not good at others, and it won't matter in the slightest when what really interests you takes hold. No need to be in a hurry, but when you find it, go with it.

Yes, you're right – the grown ups aren't always equal to the amount of power they seem to hold. They know it, too. They're following rules they don't entirely understand. Most of their self-importance is faked.

You don't have to be afraid of all of that.

There are no burglars – none that matter – and you won't be losing anyone else you know and love personally, like Marion, to a land mine.

Your dad loves you, he just doesn't know how to express it. He's proud of you, even if you can't wrestle those king rag worms onto the hook to his satisfaction. And he loves your mom, he just doesn't know how to express it. There is no lack in him or anyone that you have to make up for.

Look out for your little brother. He's not as strong as you are. He only pretends indifference.

It's not important to like everyone the same – let things take their natural course. You can trust that. . . And earth, air, fire, water and helping animals. They'll always come down on your side, even if appearances get shaky now and then.

Work is the best laboratory I know of to transform yourself and your relationship to life. You'll catch on quickly – trust yourself.

I have to warn you – being disdainful or judgmental to protect yourself from getting hurt is not going to be all that successful for you. But you don't need me to tell you that – you like to find out on your own. And like most people, you work best without too much direction.

You're a soul that likes surprises, and there'll be plenty for you to enjoy or forgive, one after another. You'll know a lot of love in your life. You are going to receive and give more love than your arms can ever hold.

You are an innocent child of God. You're a magician, not because you can make things go your way, but because you will always be alert to the miracle.

I love you. I'm looking out for you. Have fun. Sex is a good, not a bad thing. Ignore all reprimands to the contrary.

Try to consider how others might be feeling now and then. You're all interlocking parts of a great big picture puzzle, and all astounding, odd-shaped and necessary.

You shall have music wherever you go.

Love and God bless,
Ken x

Ken Russell

P.S. Those paintings you made that you suspect are dreadful are really, really, really good.

Drawing of Ken aged 16, by his wife Elize Russell

Hayley Mills

Dear Me,

A few things I've learnt, and wish I'd understood back then.

When you awake be thankful for the new day. Be grateful for everything you have in your life, the big things and the little things even the hard and difficult things, for they will be your best teachers. If you are truly grateful you can never become arrogant and proud.

Love and respect your body, it is the temple of your soul. Your health and your happiness are in your own hands.

Become a vegetarian. It's better for you and for the planet.

Never underestimate the power of your own mind, and who controls it.

Find a spiritual path that works for you, seek wisdom and truth, and always be tolerant of the paths of others.

Read, and learn, you'll never know it all. And love, love with all your heart. Love life in all its forms and complexity, love people, love all living creatures. The more you love the greater your capacity to love.

You don't need money to be happy, it helps, but you do need love.

Don't start smoking, it's hell to give up. Don't drink too much, it wrecks your health, makes you look like shit and leads you astray.

Hayley

Rolf Harris

Rolf by Rolf, 1946

RolfHarris

Dear 16 year old Rolf,

You think you're a bit special because you've won a big swimming race and you've had yourself portrait hung in a prestigious art competition, but please, don't get bigheaded. Remember that there are more important things in life. Just stay the loving kid that you are.

You're worried as to where you should look for a career. Just keep the swimming as the fun thing it's always been, but pursue the art, the music and the urge to show off, and to entertain. They could become career areas in the future. But, if you do have any success, you'll need to conquer your fear of discussing money. Learn how to handle it.

Continue to have a go at anything and everything the way your Mum and Dad encouraged you to. For example, that article you've just read describing this new phenomenon of 'television' which is sweeping America. You felt you could be good at that. Well, it won't arrive in Australia for many, many years, but when you start to

(2) travel, and you do come across it, you will get involved. It will be the answer to all your worries about career direction.

Tell your loved ones how much you love them. They won't be around for ever.

The most important thing of all is, be REAL! Don't ever get too high and mighty and stuck-up. Talk to everyone, and treat them all as equals.

Keep painting and also keep creating all those cartoons you love to draw. They will make your whole life a joy, and, by the way, here's a good cartoon signature self portrait you could use if you ever decide to grow a beard.

I love you dearly, and I'll keep telling you that!

your older self.

Dear Ozwald,

It's great you've discovered fashion is your dream. You have talent for it. But it will lead you to other things that you can't even imagine. It will seem difficult, it will be dark. You will be lost and afraid. But the fear is neccessary for you to learn because out of that fear and loss, you will achieve everything you've ever dreamed of.

Ozwald Boateng

Yoko Ono

June 22, 2009

Dear Yoko,

You are 16 and are so young to have decided to be an artist at this time in your life. First let me congratulate you on your choice. From here on, you enter the endless magic life of being an artist.

The world is your oyster: it will provide you with unlimited material for your art. Look at it again from that point of view. Suddenly the world is a different place, so interesting, so beautiful, and so mysterious. Have fun with it. And share your fun with everyone around you.

You, as an artist, will unfold the infinite mystery of life, and share it with the world. It may just be two people your work will communicate to. Don't be upset. Be upset if you are not happy with your work. Never be upset about how many people have seen it, or how many reviews it has received. Your work will exist and keep influencing the world. Moreover, your work will keep changing the very configuration of our world no matter what kind of attention it gets or it doesn't get. So even when you are an unknown artist, be caring of what you make and what you give out. Your work, no matter what, effects the world, and in return, it brings back 10 times of what you've given out. If you give out junk, you get back junk. If you give out confusion, you will give yourself confusion. If you give out something beautiful, you will get back 10 times more beauty in your life. That's how it works.

You are now like a tree in the park. Your existence is making the city breathe well. So relax and be yourself. Don't try to be anything but yourself. Rely on your instinct and inspiration. Go with it!

Believe in yourself. You will have a radiant life. I love you!

Dear Nitin,

Abstinence – exercise restraint over chocolates, sugar, sauces, falling in love, thinking too much, trusting without cynicism, cynicism without patience and meat without vegetables.

Bulerias – Practice this now – watch Paco de Lucia – learn the rhythm and play it everyday – You will get better eventually – honest!

Cartwheels – try this and don't give up. As Douglas Adams says – it's just about "throwing oneself at the ground and missing...." – only he was talking about flying which is much harder. I don't want you getting to my age and being scared of throwing yourself at the ground.

Deferred gratification – all good things will come when you enjoy the journey more than the outcome. Slow down, relax - it's ok to take your time and enjoy the moment – the past and future are illusion – live in the now. Seems obvious but it is true. Which means we're not real to each other so we probably wouldn't get on.

Education – This starts from the moment you leave school and ends the moment you stop following your intuition. Believe in your feelings – the more you do, the more attuned they become. Actually, listen to Obi Wan Kenobi on this.

Fun – Have loads of this for God's (see G) sake. It's important!

God – is very, very complicated – better concentrate on your cartwheels instead.

Higgs Boson – start looking for this now – If you find it in time you could charge 10 billion pounds to spill your guts and save physicists the bother of inventing the Large Hadron collider at Cern. Alternatively, just invent the Large Hadron Collider at Cern. I'll send you the blueprints. Everyone will be so impressed.

Indian classical music – Keep practicing, watching and playing – you can never get enough.

Jazz – Keep practicing, watching and playing – you can never get enough.

Kickboxing – start this now...er...then – by the time you're me I should be lethal – in fact, why aren't I? - Unless you haven't bothered reading this.... Lord, tenses are not easy with this stuff.

Love – Is about patience, consideration, selflessness and empathy – NOT narcissism – You know what I mean!

Music - is a universal language that transcends all boundaries - be they national, emotional, communicative, expressive, spiritual, cultural or prejudicial – start to think about that now – you'll be surprised by how much you can learn from that single fact.

Nusrat Fateh Ali Khan – Remix him before someone else does – You can't go wrong with that voice.

Obvious – Don't assume anything is.

Nitin Sawhney

Phobias – Learn about this stuff called "Cognitive Behaviourial Therapy" and also "Psychodynamic Psychology". You'll find that slowly but surely you can get past anything. Unless you come across Scientologists – in which case it's best not to mention Psychology. They don't like it.

Quantum theory – This will help you with "H" and also give you an insight into a lot of ideas behind Hinduism – In some ways, the ideas are very similar. Just switch hypothetical cats and unpredictable particles for "Dharma" and "Maya" – sort of.

Recordings – Take time to be cathartic about the past – shake, cry, play music – whatever it takes to allow bad experiences to be exorcised from your mind. Emotional recordings of the past interrupt new experiences and present-mindedness. Alternately, watch "Father Ted" – which will have a similar effect.

Skull and Bones society at Yale University - A weird cult that produces belligerent American presidents. Check it out.

Technology – Don't get too distracted by this. Easy to start thinking this is all- important when it's generally the simple things that work best – You'll find that out when you're smashing the hell out of a pc keyboard one day.

Urgent – very little is, although many will try to convince you otherwise. Take time to do things in a way that feels right.

Vedas – Read about the Vedas and the Upanishads – you will discover incredible facts about mathematics – the 16 sutras – also music, philosophy, life and.... er.... animal sacrifice.... Actually, ignore that part.

Worry – Don't – It all works out.

Xenophobia – Keep this in mind. You'll be amazed how much is in the subtext. Actually, watch out for it when this bloke called Tony Blair starts talking about Iraq after 9/11/2001 – you'll be stunned by what happens.

Yoga – watch mum – she knows a lot about how to focus mind and body – this is the most perfect way to keep your asthma in check and your energy in its natural flow. Moreover, it means you get to hang upside down a lot. You'll like that.

Zero – The chances of you handwriting and fitting all this on a single page. Don't bother trying.

Best

N.tin

Nitin & his cousins. He is 16 at the back in beige!

June 2009

A letter to Lynda

As I think back to you my 16-year-old self, I want to give you advice but am finding it hard to do so, because nothing I have ever done was on anyone else's advice. So maybe I should just encourage you to follow your dreams. If you want something badly enough and are prepared to work towards the end result, it will happen.

Looking back at you now, you're just about to get on that train from Liverpool to London to take up your RADA scholarship. Leaving that undiagnosed dyslexia and stressful schoolwork behind you, never imagining where this journey will take you. Stand by for some tough talk as you walk through the acting part of your life. The Principal of RADA will tell you that you're too small, not attractive enough and will only be a character actress who gets to work in her 40's. Don't worry though because at the stage door of The Liverpool Playhouse in a few years time, you'll get the chance to tell him to f off, in between bows for your role as a Goldoni beauty opposite Anthony Hopkins. That will feel good.

Acting will be the first thing you succeed at although never your great passion, but it will lead you to your destiny so try to trust in that. During filming on The Gentle Touch in your 30s with Jill Gascoine you'll ask to submit some stories that might be a little less boring, and you won't know quite what possessed you to do so. You'll probably remember your father keeping that small note, written by Lynda Titchmarsh, with a story about "a norty girl who stoal a bisycle and fel of it" and reflect on how you've always been a storyteller really.
You won't get any of those stories accepted, but you will treasure the comment written across one of them "This is Brilliant", and use it to spur you on. You will rewrite that story, rename it Widows and send it to a producer you know called Verity Lambert and you will use your married name Lynda La Plante (and you will laugh when she says that she thought that sounded like a transvestite trucker!)

You will get a series commissioned, realise that you don't know what on earth to do now and find inspiration and direction through the power of research and talking to the people you're trying to write. The buzz you will get from building the script will be more enjoyable than anything you've done before, and that's when you'll know that you've found what you want to do for your whole life. You'll find that writing will lead you to producing TV, that TV will lead you to novels and that you will still, years on, love what you do.

Lynda La Plante

May you never cease to be amazed at the support of the fans and the level of your success. May you leave no stone unturned and fight for what you want in a script because you'll never stop having to do so. May you always have belief in and respect for yourself and know that work is pleasure. May you feel as I do now that every day is special, and despite the heartaches (and you will have them) you will see that they are miniscule compared to your constant joy at being able to earn your living doing exactly what you find fulfilling.

Love to you Lynda, from

PS, just remembered

You hate queuing, you always will, so learn to get everywhere early, be it Legoland with your darling son or any other such unthinkable place.

Be organised, it really does work in reducing stress and allows you to enjoy life to the max.

Don't worry about diets, you will never be able to sustain one for more than a few days.

Finally try not to smoke, drink yes in moderation but don't start smoking whatever you do. If anyone asks, tell them it's because you don't want all those little lines around your mouth!

by Stephen Berkoff

Dear Me   Tehran 30 June 2009

Life is going to be good in the next few years. You're lucky – you come from a happy family, your parents love you and you have some excellent friends.

What you don't have at the moment is a girlfriend. That doesn't bother you, but I think you would quite like to have one.

The truth is that you need to have more confidence with girls. I am looking at the picture of you and frankly you're not too bad. Why don't you ask Jane Jeffreys out? She might even say yes.

Don't worry about the way your brothers will try to make it embarrassing. So what if you turn slightly red? Just laugh pityingly the next time Nicholas and Matthew grab pieces of bread and hold them up to your face shouting 'toast! toast!' if your face heats up a bit when someone asks you about a girl.

By the way it is not always necessary to get pissed first before you talk to them. You are going to make a few girl breakthroughs before you're 17 (minor success, so don't get too excited).

Now for some advice you might prefer not to hear.

Work a bit harder on foreign languages. Stop taking perverse pride in being bad at French. Arabic might be useful in the future. Don't look so surprised.

Do sit-ups. At 16 you like playing rugby, even though you are not all that talented, so you're quite fit. When you get to university in a few years, you more or less give up doing any sport at all. So work harder to keep fit. Or it will be agony when you start again from scratch in your 30s.

When you're 16 it's hard to imagine what it's like to be 20, let alone 49 as we are now. But as you get older time will speed up, so pack in as much as you can as soon as you can. And make choices. Don't drift.

You realise that there is a big world out there, and you want to be part of it. Don't wait until you take a year off before you go to university. Start now.

Try hitching to Paris and back. When eventually you do a big trip you will be more home sick than you imagined, so do some long weekends away to see how it feels.

I'm not sure it's necessary to lecture you like this, because I think you realise most of it anyway.

Just enjoy life, and work hard (you could work harder at school than you do) and you are not going to mess up too much.

It's going to be great…!

Jeremy

Jeremy Bowen

July 15, 2009

Dear Suzy,

Here's what I have to say to you, a sixteen-year-old girl; things will work out beyond what you can imagine, although not everything will happen as you might like it to, or expect it to be. What you've learned so far will serve you well. The things you believe in really are good, so don't change your values! The things you think are stupid really are stupid; violence and injustice, for example, especially against women and children, but against any individual.

Keep learning, and don't be cynical. You can't change the world by yourself, but you have a lot more power than you ever thought possible to touch people. Don't worry if you blend into the crowd. Sometimes that's more important than standing out in one. What are people feeling? Feel what people feel, and put it into words. Don't just focus on yourself.

Some of your problems will stay with you your whole life, and fame or success won't change that. The struggle to be disciplined never gets easier. Fame and success don't buy contentment or inner balance. Eventually you will be happier with yourself, and you won't struggle against your own nature. Hopefully! Enjoy yourself more! Have confidence! Let yourself love and be loved.

Love,
Suzanne Vega

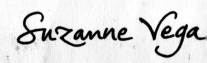

Dear Me—

Well, if you're reading this, time travel is possible, so that should please you. It's 1982 where you are and, as I recollect, that's fine. Great bands. Sunshine. Thunderbird wine. Jumble-sale overcoats and a fringe so long it pokes you in the eye. Everywhere: dayglo, leg-warmers, Chris Biggins glasses. 2009 isn't so different.

Now then — advice. You are a gay. You've known this forever. Since you had a crush on Stuart Damon off 'The Champions'. Bar one long afternoon of denial, you are perfectly content with this.

Don't be in such a hurry to grow up. Plenty of time for that. So, don't blow your first wage packet on a tailor-made tweed suit.

Mark Gatiss

You don't know it but you're living in the Dark Ages. Things will improve radically. One day, your family will come to your wedding to another man & declare it one of the happiest times of their lives. The future, though, is no Utopia. Battles we thought won are being fought again. Ignorance & fanaticism are on heat. Plenty of surprises to come — good & bad. Thatcher will go one day as, alas, will most of your hair. For now, enjoy that wonderful teenage bubble where you can cause a minor scandal by snogging the cooler-than-the-Fonz Brian Bennett. Even if you never do anything about that blond 6th former (no, honestly, he _is_) it's been nice catching up.

Just promise me that when you meet Al Murray at the Edinburgh Festival in a few years you'll have a stern word. Ok?

Love Mole x

Dr Christian Jessen

General
Medical
CLINICS

Baker Street Medical Centre

20th June 2009

My dear Christian,

What an odd chap you are. Forgive the presumption of me writing to you and thinking I can be of help. You only ever do your own thing anyway but as I'm now twice your age I do have a slight head start on you.

Unlike most teens you're not full of anger, pain, shame and angst. You are actually quite happy I think. But that's because you absolutely refuse to fit in. You won't adopt the latest trend, you won't get enthusiastic about a new pop group, and whilst smoking and sport are de rigueur at your school you stubbornly refuse to do either. And so the pressure felt by other kids to keep up with their peers is unfelt by you and you glide on by. But be told: you are maddeningly difficult. Being an only child has made you stubborn, inflexible, selfish and egocentric and only an angel schooled in limitless tolerance could possibly put up with you. Thankfully you meet one.

Your tendency to do exactly the opposite to everyone else, to never jump through hoops and never approach things by the usual channels will frustrate many, especially your parents, but stick to it. It does seem to work for you. You have one great advantage –you understand people, which at your age means knowing how to deal with adults. This opens many doors. I know your grandmother nags you to distraction about manners, she did me too but she is absolutely right to. I don't have her around anymore so listen to her for me (if you could persuade her to take half an aspirin a day, starting now, she might still be here.) Courtesy, kindness and not using a fruit knife to butter your bread will be the key to winning over many useful contacts, as will flirting outrageously, but you have already worked that one out.

If would be great if you could resist the temptation to pierce bits of you. I know it's all to do with your self confidence and I know you hate the way you look now but you will grow into your awkward, gangly body and long face. You just haven't quite worked out who you are yet. That's about to happen in a few months when you fall in love for the first time. Be warned that this will be the most horrible and agonisingly painful thing you have yet experienced; that I have yet experienced come to think of it. Considering that one day you develop appendicitis which you then manage to ignore for so long that it ruptures and gives you a life-threatening peritonitis, that's saying something. This looming love will be worse, a hundred thousand times worse. It won't lead anywhere, you won't end up like they do in the movies and it will hurt, hurt, hurt. But it will fill in the last few missing pieces of who you are, so don't fight it.

By the way, what they told you about a career in the theatre –that you can always go back to it when you finish your medical degree is a huge porkie pie and they know it. You won't go back. But medicine's not so bad and surprisingly it will give you a chance to perform. I know you are going to have fun. I still am.

Christian x

Uni
bakerst

General Medical Clinics PLC. Registered office 2-3 Salisbury Co

Little Miss Jocelyn

London June 2009

DEAR ME

Dear Jossy,

How are you? Sorry I haven't been in touch for sooooooo long; things have been quite full on for me and I didn't think you would want to hear from me. I know you sometimes have a problem listening to people of authority, but as I've been through exactly the same things as you, I thought I'd write to help you out. So here's a list [you love those]:

[1] The reason why you love LA LAW, CASUALTY and THE A-TEAM isn't because you want to be a lawyer, doctor or negotiator, it's because you want to play those parts because you want to become an actor. So don't put "doctor" on your work experience form, because they'll pack you off to boots!

[2] It's ok to talk to yourself, dream, invent scenarios and act them out with yourself; it's all part of developing your imagination, which you're gonna need.

[3] Make sure you collect all of your art work otherwise they'll burn it and then you'll be forced to call your art teacher a senile old git.

[4] It's ok to read every single Mills And Boon book ever written, it's even better when you skip most of it and go straight for the juicy bits! THEY ARE SO ROMANTIC!

[5] Hold onto your friend ESTHER, you'll be friends forever!

[6] You'll never be like Janet Jackson so STOP PUTTING ~~FUCKING~~ CHEMICALS IN YOUR HAIR! You've cost me a fortune in salon appointments!

[7] Well done for balancing "goody" Jossy with "misunderstood and completely blameless" Jossy.

[8] GOOD NEWS FLASH: You WILL grow into your nose!

That's it [for now]. Apart from all of the above, keep doing what you're doing, enjoy life and keep smiling - it's great for your facial muscles!

Lots of wiser love [only just] Joss x x x

Jocelyn x

P.S Your tits are gonna be MASSIVE!

1 - 7 - 09

Dear Tracey,

Some of this may upset you. But I feel
I have to be honest.

1) Just because you are hurt and broken.
and don't trust any one – This dose not
give you an excuse to lash out and
always be on the attack.

2) You are a beautiful natural girl. So why
do you dye your hair Jet black – And where
so much make up and hair spray.

3) You must eat – It may seem cool to
like a mini Vampire – but I asure you
it is not.

4) You have been homeless for a year now.
I feel so sorry for you. But you must have
Faith that one day everything will be ok.
This is just a tempary situation.

5) Why dont you try to go back into Education
get some qualifications – Try to go to
Universatie.

6) You are very artistic and creative.
maybe you should try to go to Art School.

Tracey Emin

7) Look into your Local Adult Education centre - See if there are any classes you can do.

8) I am not lecturing you - I just want you to know there is a whole world out there - This is not the end It is just the beginning.

9) Sometimes I can see you have been crying - I can see you are afraid. But you are are strong - and a very funny girl. Keep smiling and you will get through all of this -

10) One day in the Future I hope we can meet again and I know your life will be good.

All my Love
Tracey Emin

Jane Fonda

JANE FONDA

Beverly Hills, CA

June 2009

Dear Jane,

I know that no one has let you know that it's all right to say "no." I know that despite your considerable attributes (you tell good stories; you are brave and fair; you do not lie; you are attractive—a bit awkward, but attractive) you think you have to do what others want you to do so they will like you. You don't know it, but I've been watching for quite a while now and I don't like seeing you give yourself away. You remind me of a colander. Do you know what a colander is? It's a bowl full of holes that people use to drain food. Instead of holding yourself all together as people do who believe they have value, you let yourself drain away. The opposite of this draining is what's called agency. Agency means you listen to your body and to your heart. If you don't feel safe, if your muscles are tight and your breathing shallow, you walk away instead of ignoring those signals and going along so people will like you and won't know how scared you are.

I believe that one day in the future, if you've learned to value your intrinsic self, you will look back and remember the girl you are today and feel great compassion for her. You will feel angry with the people who should have made you feel loveable and then you will forgive them because you will understand that they did the best they could. And once you have forgiven them, everything will come together for you.

In the meantime, practice standing on your own two feet and saying 'no' when you feel like it.

With Love,

May 2009.

Dear Me,

Well look at you - out there in the big world already. Your ambition and drive is admirable. Your sense of fun and your need to give and receive love is endearing.

I know you will not want a load of advice from me, but as I have your full attention I'm going to give it anyway.

Try and love yourself for the right reasons, not to fuel your ego, but to feed your soul. Trust your family, and set firm boundaries with friends, always be kind to those who truly love you. Don't lose sight of your spirituality. Try not to set your dreams in stone. The universe will bring the challenges you need, that are necessary for your growth. Believe in your abilities - don't be too hard on yourself. Don't allow fear and insecurity to take over - both will create awkward obstacles on your life-path. Now - this is a tough one! Try not to fall so deeply in love with your romantic partners. You have so much to do in life, so learn how to be happy in your own company, without relying on someone else to fill the void in your heart.

Always observe and respect your feelings, find ways to express them appropriately, if ignored it will take years to unravel them later on in life - believe me, I know!

Have fun, make the most of every second. Live just for today. Have no regrets. Remember, if you live life well in the present, you will have a beautiful past to look back on.

Love, light and happiness

Me
xxx

doghouse-media.co.uk

Julia Sawalha

London 2009,

Dear Ann,

You don't realize it yet, but very soon, the name "Ann" will become redundant. Most people will call you Annie, and "Ann" will be a thing of the past. Getting a place at the Royal Academy of Music is not to be sniffed at, but you're going to be very unhappy there, and spend the next three years feeling pretty miserable, lost and confused. You're also going to cut a swathe through Bedsit land every six months, and it's not going to get much better..... for years. True.... £3 a week isn't much to live on.

Better get used to it though girl, it's not going to improve much for a long time.

There are mainly "frogs" actually — almost totally. Don't even bother thinking about kissing them. They'll still be frogs.

Stupid, selfish, idiotic, egocentric, arrogant, narcissistic, hardcore frogs..... with almost no exceptions.

But, you know what? You're going to write a lot of songs about how miserable, sad & confused that made you feel, and a lot of people will "get it" so you'll survive it in the end.

Annie Lennox

You'll never live in Scotland again, but you will travel the world and the seven seas in vans, cars, buses, trains and airplanes. You'll make a lot of mistakes, and do a lot of things you'll regret, but you will lead many interesting lives.... and you'll go through a thousand shades of weather every day!

You will learn that EVERYTHING changes, and you'll realize that "everything" "is a certain kind of illusion in any case.

You'll have massive gains and massive losses, and you'll learn that bitterness only corrodes the vessel that it contains.

You'll learn to love unconditionally.... (excluding the gremolins!)

lots of love from Annie

Annie

Fay Weldon

Dorset, 2009.

Dear Fay, back then –

Stop worrying. There is nothing wrong with you. Your family is totally nuts but you are perfectly sane. You are living with your mother and your sister in one room in North London, and have had to spend the day in bed to keep warm, the year being 1947 and this being the famous freeze. You've come from New Zealand, the land of plenty, to this grey grisly city only months after World War II ended, and if you feel a little confused it is not surprising. You may also be feeling hungry too. There's whale meat for dinner and the butter ration is less than 50 grams a week. Get used to it. You're going to be on one diet or another for the rest of your life anyway. There'll even come a time when you'll eat nothing but cabbage for days of your own free will. And by the way if you go up the road to Belsize Park Underground Station (slogan on the posters: It's Warmer Underground) and stand in the doorway – they won't let you in without a ticket – a blast of hot air comes out every two minutes as a train passes through. Join the little clutch of excluded shiverers standing outside: it's friendly and companionable. Smokers today have the same experience.

You've no mirror other than a tiny one above the basin in the communal bathroom, but I promise you, you don't look too bad. A bit stunned, probably. And not as good as your big sister but things will get better. Everything is going to get better. You're going to get a scholarship to a good school. And your mother is gong to get a job as a live-in cook/housekeeper and there'll be three rooms instead of one even if you do have to share it with a rat. And University is free and they'll even give you money to live on while you're there. It feels like wealth. And never coming first in class, but only ever second or third, doesn't mean you're stupid just that there's always someone in the world cleverer than you are. Learn this. And you will always have really good friends. Enjoy them.

No use telling you to try and marry a banker because that's not your style – your style is bohemian: folk singers, artists, poets. Face it. And no, it's not that your legs are unusually short, just that your sister's are longer. And by the way, it's all very well to want to be loved for your mind alone, but your habit of dressing like Miss Phoebe in the school production of J.M. Barrie's Quality Street when you were fourteen [see illustration] buttoned up at neck and wrists, will do you no favours. There's a lot to said for showing a bit more flesh. Since you have it, flaunt it.

Blessings – and remember to send messages back to yourself in the past, like this one now –

Fay in the future.

Dear Ryan,

First things first, it gets better.

You get better, the world is fairer and all that talking you're doing and all those sports classes you are avoiding, that's all fine too, it all stands to you in the end.

You are 16, not at all successful with the girls and, essentially, you haven't a clue about way too many things for a fellow your age. The handsome guys are doing all the scoring both on and off the pitch and I'm afraid you are just a spectator, both on and off the pitch but fear not. It gets better.

Being a teenager is a pain in the ass but you are happy enough embracing your inner nerd, not a geek (you've no interest in chess or computers, we both know that) but you are a nerd and that'll stand to you too. For the moment, you are a victim of the tyranny of beauty that is the rule of law at your age. Hang in there my man, it gets better.

Talk to your brothers and sisters a little more, they matter more than you think or know. Hug your folks, there's great love there too. Keep reading those books but stop reading the Murder Casebook magazines, that's just weird, no wonder you can't meet a girl (although being at an all-boys school doesn't help matters).

Go fishing, enjoy that first Guinness, keep cracking the gags despite them being rather unfunny and keep talking, always keep talking.

I have regrets but you'll see them coming this time. You also have extraordinary good fortune, exciting opportunities and two little girls waiting for you with arms as wide as the grins on their beautiful faces.

You mope a bit, get a bit spotty and have really dodgy Jason Donovon hair but you have to believe me, it gets better.

Read, laugh, flirt, hug, love, mess, indulge your quirks and keep your family close.

Until then young man,

The elder lemon.

Emma Thompson

Dear Em (16)

May 29th
2009

I realise that you are young and in love and
that nothing much that anyone old says seems
relevant, but seeing as it's me — that is, you.
That is, us, I think it's worth a go.

Two Top Tips from 50 to 16:

1) Don't EVER EVER EVER bother to go on a diet.
I know you're obsessed and have that awful thing
of standing in the 6th form canteen trying to choose
between a yoghurt & a breathe of fresh air (whilst
wanting chips & a cheese salad). Don't sweat it.
Eat regularly, try & avoid rubbish and never diet.
You'll end up the same size anyway, so drop it girl, +
drop it NOW. Believe me — nobody cares. Diets are
the best way of confusing your metabolism for the
rest of your life. Just be you + get on with it
I cannot tell you how much time + energy you'll
save + how much happier you'll be.

2) When he says he doesn't love you, believe him.
He doesn't.

That's it. All the other mistakes you
make are worth their weight in gold.

I love you — Em (50)

Dear James,

Stay in more, keep off the smokes and tell your parents you love them.

James Nesbitt

James Nesbitt

Dear Libby,

Sixteen! You've got A levels looming, and they'll make you give things up to concentrate on them: notably your flute lessons and your judo. Dig your heels in and refuse: by the time you get to be my age, educationalists will have realized that music and sport actually enhance academic learning. As well as making you happier. And you need to be happier. You'll regret giving up your instrument, not to mention the therapeutic benefits of getting into loose canvas pyjamas and hurling people around on a mat. Tell them NO.

Never mind. There are other lessons you could take to heart right now, if only you'd listen. As a good diplo-brat, trained since child-hood to hand round vol-au-vents and make decorous small talk with adults, you think yourself grown-up. Well, you're not. That veneer of social competence will crack when you get out of boarding school and embassy life into the maelstrom of student freedom, and when it does you'll be gauche, way out of your depth in the swinging sixties, horrifyingly emotionally vulnerable, prone to fall in love with quite the wrong chaps. Never mind, it'll be quite fun really.

Two things to remember. Enjoy ordinary pleasures while they're happening - wood-pigeons cooing, a picnic, a walk, a moonlit walk home up the Edgware Road from yet another disastrous party. And know this: the cool people, the sorted, the fashionable, the ones you think far above you, are not really all that confident either. Be nice to them. Give them a hug. Respond to them as human beings, not icons. They may not despise you quite as much as you assume. Even if they do, there are plenty more where they came from. You need human beings around you, and of those there is no shortage.

good luck
L

Dear Hugh (age 16),

My advice to you is to learn to say no to things that simply cannot be done properly in the limited time available.

Yours,

Hugh (age 44)

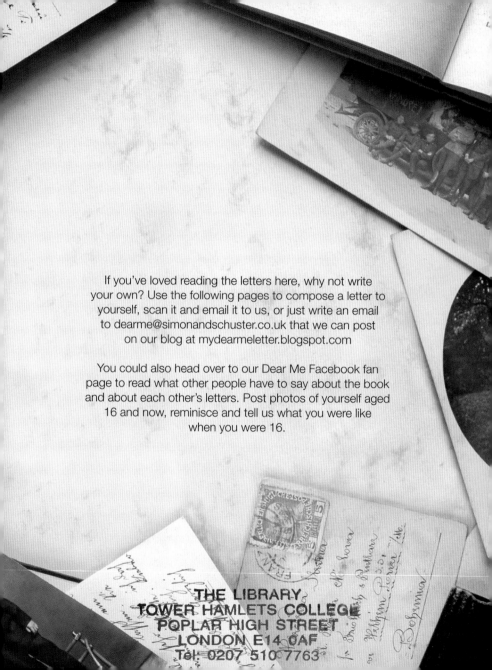

If you've loved reading the letters here, why not write your own? Use the following pages to compose a letter to yourself, scan it and email it to us, or just write an email to dearme@simonandschuster.co.uk that we can post on our blog at mydearmeletter.blogspot.com

You could also head over to our Dear Me Facebook fan page to read what other people have to say about the book and about each other's letters. Post photos of yourself aged 16 and now, reminisce and tell us what you were like when you were 16.

THE LIBRARY
TOWER HAMLETS COLLEGE
POPLAR HIGH STREET
LONDON E14 0AF
Tel: 0207 510 7763

.... *aged 16 years of age*

Acknowledgements

The editors wish to send a huge thank-you to all the contributors:
you have been generous with your time and imaginations and have
made this project a joy to work on.

Special thanks goes to: Simon Prytherch at the Elton John AIDS Foundation,
who has been a pleasure to work with, gave the book legs and moved
the goalposts brilliantly.

Extra special thanks to Nigel Stoneman: commissioning editor,
co-compiler, publicist extraordinaire and great friend.

Letters of commendation and gratitude to everyone who has so generously
given of their time, help and support in so many different ways, in no particular
order and with apologies to the people we have undoubtedly missed:

Mike Jones, Liane Payne, Rob Cox, Rafaela Romaya. Gary Farrow, Patrick
Strudwick, Henry Jeffreys, Sue Main, Kelly Weiss, Gavin Barker, Tim Teeman,
Fleur Saunders-Davies, Alexandra Hill, Michelle Bega, Julia Holdway, Antony
Topping, Joyce Burnett, Tara Mallett, Jo Crocker, Georgia Glover, Laura
Halls, Vicki Claffey, Gary Reich, Ian Johnson, Joyce Deen, Richard Cain, Joan
Marshrons, Murray Chalmers, Amanda Keeley, Chetna Bhatt, Vivienne Clore,
Mark Adderley, Denne Dempsey, Tina Arena, Viv Irish, Lisa Thomas, Louise
Page, Faye Anthony, Colin Davies, Paul Mills, Michael Hausman, Charlie
Fotheringham, Mark King, Dave Aussenberg, Steven Bennett, Jennifer Abel,
Adriana Trigiani, Merrilee Heifetz, Melody Korenbrot, Bob Henderson,
Joe Heaney, Noel Kelly, Niamh Kirwan, Tanya Nathan, Georgie Gibbon,
Anton Monsted, Lee Randall, Nick Boyles, Richard Dobbs, Charlotte
Robertson, Debi Allen, Tim Quayle, Chris Paling, Robert Smith, Nick Fox,
Tamu Matose, Will Hollinshead, Emma Harrow, Rose Lloyd Owen,
Nick Southall, Louisa McGillicuddy, Pat Lake-Smith, Carol Barrowman,
Alison Parker, Michelle Benson, Noel Kelly, Emma, Andy and Finn Seager,
the Gallianos, the O'Neils and Mark Stuart Doig… without whom.

ELTON JOHN AIDS FOUNDATION

The Elton John AIDS Foundation (EJAF) in the UK is an international non-profit organisation funding programmes that help to alleviate the physical, emotional and financial hardship of those living with, affected by or at risk of HIV/AIDS.

EJAF was formed primarily to look after the needs of people with HIV/AIDS living in the United Kingdom. During the past sixteen years, the organisation has extended the scope of its work and now funds in 15 countries over 4 continents.

To date it has raised over £65 million which has been used to support more than 1,100 projects reaching millions of people infected, affected or at risk of HIV/AIDS including:

- Providing information about HIV/AIDS to over 150 million people around the globe, including 5 million children.
- Giving 185,000 people with AIDS in South Africa, often dying alone and in pain, proper palliative care.
- Putting 10,000 adults on antiretroviral treatment in Sub-Saharan Africa.
- Supporting more than 57,000 people in need to access income generation programmes, vocational training, grants or loans.
- Enabling over 200,000 people living with HIV/AIDS to be supported through positive people's groups & networks

EJAF is proud of its record of championing innovative programmes, including helping to spearhead the global expansion of HIV/AIDS treatment & care, most recently paediatric antiretroviral treatment; being one of the first grant makers in the world to acknowledge the needs of men who have sex with men (MSM) in countries where homosexuality is still illegal; supporting needle exchange and methadone substitution programmes for injecting drug users living with or at risk of HIV/AIDS.

The office in London has overheads running under 5% and is staffed by five full-time and six part-time members of staff, helped by two volunteers.

For further information on the charity please go to: www.ejaf.com